D1486163

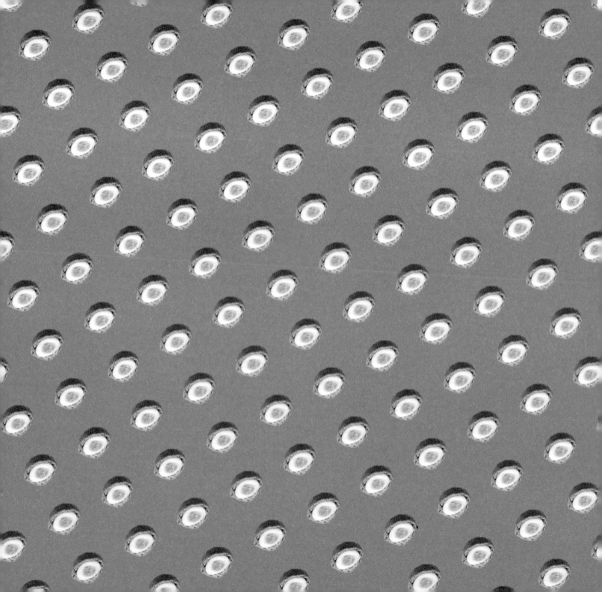

A PRAT'S PROGRESS

COLD WAR STEVE

PRESENTS...

A PRAT'S PROGRESS

 Thames & Hudson

I'd like to thank Andrew Sanigar, Sophie Mead and Nick Jakins at Thames
& Hudson. My mom (Charlotte) and dad (Peter), Matt, Jimbob and Mel,
Theresa and Alan, Emma, Elora and Mark, Paul, Amy and Lorian.

Massive thank you to my manager/Svengali/midfield-general Carl Gosling,
who is the reason everything has taken off the way it has.

Finally a special thank you to my wife Katy, who despite working long
hours at a care home (in her words 'wiping old people's arses') does
everything to ensure I'm able to get stuff done and is the most amazing
mom to our beautiful girls Isabelle, Sophie and Evie and new arrival, Toby
the Lithuanian sausage dog.

(cover) Untitled, design by Nick Jakins
(pages 2–3) Yacht-Cocks
(opposite) Street Party
(page 128) Boris Johnson's Homemade Bus

First published in the United Kingdom in 2019 by Thames & Hudson Ltd,
181A High Holborn, London WC1V 7QX

Cold War Steve Presents ...A Prat's Progress © 2019 Thames & Hudson Ltd, London

Illustrations and Captions © 2019 Christopher Spencer
Introduction © 2019 Christopher Spencer

British Library Cataloguing-in-Publication Data
A catalogue record for this book is available from the British Library

ISBN 978-0-500-02342-6

Printed and bound in Slovenia by DZS-Grafik d.o.o.

To find out about all our publications, please visit
www.thamesandhudson.com. There you can subscribe
to our e-newsletter, browse or download our current
catalogue, and buy any titles that are in print.

INDEPENDENCE DAY

HAPPY INDEPENDENCE DAY
29 MARCH 2019

Introduction

BY CHRISTOPHER SPENCER

Y ou may be reading this decades from now — an odd little book you unearthed while clearing out your great-aunt's lean-to (under several cans of unused suede and nubuck renovator spray). It's possible you are using it as primary evidence for your history homework; a two thousand word essay on 'what the actual fuck happened to the formerly United Kingdom in the years 2016 to 2020, which led to England becoming an isolated fascist state, dominated by gangs of quad-biking, ruddy-cheeked young farmers, in yellow jumbo cords and wax jackets, whooping and terrorising towns and cities, in their barbarous hunt for tinned meat products?'

In the interest of balance, I should also add that the essay you're required to write, could well be 'what happened to the United Kingdom in the years 2016 to 2020, which led to these endless sunlit uplands, halcyon days and prosperity for all?'

While this book is admittedly not as significant as say, Daniel Defoe's *Journal of the Plague Year*, I hope it provides you with an enlightening pictorial account of these perturbing times. You may be confused by some of the scenes, but I can assure you that they accurately reflect the absurdity of our current disposition.

A PRAT'S PROGRESS

It was the publishers (or more specifically the wife of Commissioning Editor Andrew Sanigar) who came up with the title of the book — a take on William Hogarth's series of eight paintings, *A Rake's Progress*. Alexander Boris de Pfeffel Johnson is the 'prat' whose progress is ostensibly documented here. There is an uneasy informality in referring to our current Prime Minister (at the time of writing at least) by his first name only. To do so colludes with the bullshit, chummy, bumbling, affable bloke-of-the people bollocks. So I won't.

Alexander Boris de Pfeffel Johnson's quest to be Prime Minister, by whatever means necessary, at whatever cost to the

United Kingdom, is now complete. We have triumphantly 'taken back control' — a Prime Minister put into power by 0.13% of the population, an unelected goblin (Dominic Cummings) pulling all the strings and an insistence that 'no deal' is what everyone voted for in the first place. There's Trump in the White House, Steve Bannon being allowed to exert his far-right flatulence upon willing international governments, the existence of the Brexit Party and the people in it and right-wing, tax-avoiding media tycoons and disaster capitalists continuing to manipulate huge swathes of the country. Perhaps most distressing of all is the continued rise of fascism, bigotry and gammonism. That and farty, sweaty little men such as Mark Gino Francois being given a media platform (and a step ladder) to spout their obnoxious drivel.

On reflection, the titular 'prat' could very well be me. Which is fair enough. In terms of my own progress, it's been an incredible year; exhibitions, commissions (being asked to do the front cover of *Time* magazine was insane), a collaboration with the amazing Led by Donkeys at Glastonbury, interviews, print sales, and now a second book! I am conscious of the position I find myself in; of being one of the few people to actually benefit from Brexit. I tell myself that I would swap all this — and go back to the just-above-minimum-wage job — to return to the Britain of Danny Boyle's sublime London 2012 Olympics opening ceremony. I am eternally grateful that my audience (particularly on Twitter) are so supportive, insightful and hilarious. Twitter is still my canvas of choice and the feedback and engagement there is without doubt the most rewarding element of being Cold War Steve.

My work has evolved from DIY punk cut 'n' paste bus journey pieces, to grandiose prog rock numbers that take hours to complete. The early works had an immediacy and charm, but were made to be viewed on nothing bigger than a small phone screen. I now try to create each picture as an artistic composition in its own right — a satirical piece, which makes a statement, but that people would also like a nice print of! I've taken my Bosch, Bruegel and Hogarth influences to the next level and used some of their masterpieces as backdrops — several of which are included in this book. I am intrigued by the disjunction of backdrops from the past (be it a medieval Bosch hell-scape, or a 1970s pub car park) with contemporary notables and ne'er-do-wells.

In this age of political turmoil and fat lying racists, I feel very fortunate that I am able to channel my despair into my art. I don't know what I'd be doing without it to be honest

— probably necking a litre bottle of cheap vermouth in a shopping centre toilet cubicle, while listening attentively for any other toilet users, then flush, gobble a handful of Extra Strong Mints (or Hall's Mentho-Lyptus), sheepishly emerge from the cubicle, quickly wrap the empty bottle in hand towels and put it in the bin, wash hands, look up into the mirror... and be hit by a crashing wave of self-hatred and biliousness.

August 2019

WORKS

Remnants

The Shoezone Speeches

Egg

The March to Leave

None of that Foreign Muck

The Words of a Prophet are Written in Condensation on the Window of the 11c

Ghosts of the Future

Fete

Festerval

Stepping Out

Miscreants' Retreat

Whited Sepulchres

New Faces

'Ooo Percy'

The West is Massive Sports Direct Mugs

Sausage in a Launderette

'Look Marguerite, England!'

The Unending Disappointments of Italia 90

Henman Hell

Today at Wimbledon

Blind D Date

Canteen of Cutlery

Eggheads

Catchphrase

Flying Buttress

The Ceramic White Tiger in the Window of an Amusement Arcade

The Anatomy Lesson

'We're going to get a great deal'

Scotch Egg Billiards

Chequers

Bank Holiday

Rog

Beach

Street Party Part Two

The Ivy

No Actual Boats

House of Commons Returns After the Summer Recess

> God bless the people
of Tunbridge Wells
and its environs
>God bless Peter
Beardsley and
Stephen Mulhern

Addressing the Nation

Howztwat

Center Parcs

OPPOSITE: 'Just what is it that makes today's caravans so different, so appealing?'

The Sins of the Father Are to Be Laid Upon the Children

Live Freaks

OPPOSITE: Jailhouse Cocks

The Motel Room Sausage Drone Incident

Spectres of the Future Haunting Endearing Television Programmes of my Childhood

Café Terrace Twats. At Night

OPPOSITE: Humours of an Election

Quest Presents 'Border Force UK'

Netherlandish Proverbs

Visitation of the Great White Worm

Geoff

The Bust

Melania

Ship of Twats

David Davis's Moronic Pre-Referendum Statement, About German Car Manufacturers and a UK-German Deal.

Cunts in the Snow

Another Dispiriting
Sunday Evening

Brexit Pursued by Bears
(original Bungles)

Raft of the Twats

Hey Wayne

The Winter of Discontent, Hatching from the Secretory Glands of Children Not Yet Born

PAGES 90/91: 'And when did you last see your saboteur?'

Northern Rail

Kilroy

These Are Your Lies

The Corned Beef Maze

Gourd of the Twats

OPPOSITE: Blankety Blank

FLANGE

SAM   ANNE   SAJID

DONALD   THORA

The Triumph of Death

Shitehawks

Husting

Roger Stone Waiting for his Eels and Pies

Cabinet

'What the fuck is happening?'

'Leak this'
'But it's old'
'No-one gives a shit'

Pie Rolling Two

Cocks Fight

Harridan Devouring Democracy

'I make buses'

116

Autumn Watch

Monet's Garden

Dunkirk Spirit

Prisoners Exercising

Magister Ludi

(We Don't Need This) Fascist Groove Thang

Corned
Beef
£6.99

Frijj Magnets

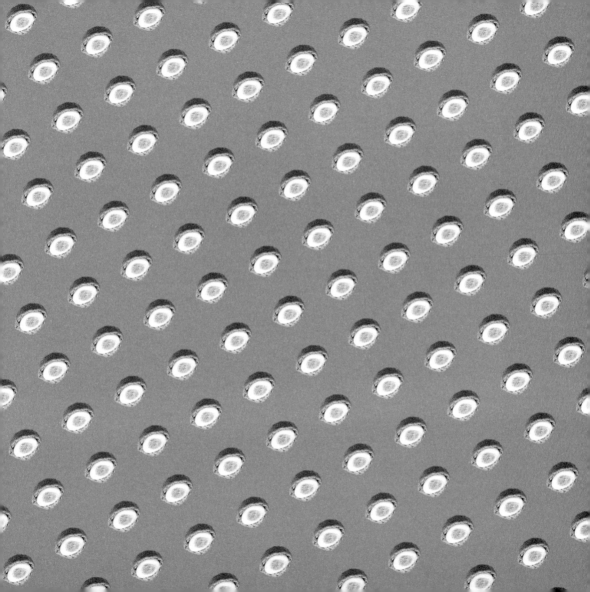

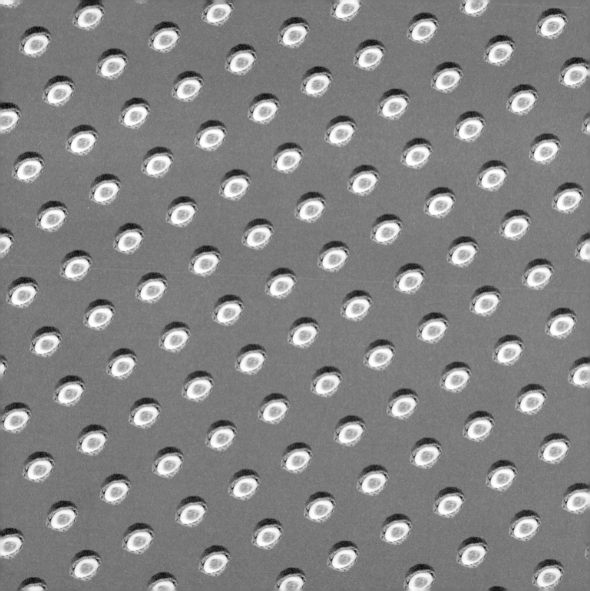